THOSE
MYSTERIOUS   DINOSAURS

A Biblical Study for children,
their parents and their teachers

by
Norma A. Whitcomb

Illustrated by Heather Harting Job

Whitcomb Ministries, Inc.
Post Office Box 277
Winona Lake, Indiana 46590

ISBN: 0-9635049-0-8
Second Printing, July 1993

DEDICATION

To our grandchildren:
Jessica, Jill, Jocelyn, David, Jamie, Laura, Janessa,
Weston, John, Kelsey, Morgan and Josiah

and any more that may be added to our quiver

and to those thousands of children who have enthusiastically
thanked me for teaching them about
"Those Mysterious Dinosaurs."

ABOUT THE AUTHOR

Mrs. Norma A. Whitcomb was reared in a Christian home in Kingston, New York, and was active in the youth and music ministries of her church.

She spent eleven years as a missionary in the Philippines with her husband, Robert Pritchett, and their two sons. Robert died in 1969, and in 1971 Mrs. Whitcomb was married to a widower, Dr. John C. Whitcomb, who had four children. For several years she was the mother of six teenagers.

Mrs. Whitcomb has served as a teacher in both public and Christian schools, as a teacher and counselor at Far Eastern Bible Institute and Seminary in the Philippines, and as an art teacher. She presently teaches ladies' Bible classes, speaks at ladies' seminars and conferences, and speaks to children about the Biblical and scientific facts concerning dinosaurs.

Mrs. Whitcomb received an A.B. degree from Houghton College, and an M.S. degree in educational guidance and counseling from Emporia State University.

Dr. and Mrs. Whitcomb have six children and ten grandchildren. Their home is in Winona Lake, Indiana.

TABLE OF CONTENTS

"The world was made through [Jesus Christ], and the world did not know Him."

JOHN 1:10

ACKNOWLEDGMENTS

I wish to thank Paulette Sauders for her many helpful suggestions when this book was in its incipient stages; and Miriam Pacheco and Norma Stech, who read the manuscript to the children in their classrooms and provided me with their feedback.

I also thank Jack Wyrtzen and Barbara Davoll who encouraged me with letters and phone calls. Dr. Gary Parker, a noted creation scientist, and his wife, Mary, clarified several scientific problems. A special thanks to Karen Eiler, who urged me to "take the completion road" when I was ready to abandon the project. Karen also generously offered her editing skills in order to help bring the book to completion. Heather Harting Job, the artist for the cover and illustrations, was a joy to work with. I want to thank Dan Elkins for preparing the camera-ready copy.

Many friends around the world have prayed. Without their support I could not have done this. And to my dear husband, John, I am gratefully indebted, because he clarified my many scientific questions about dinosaurs. He continues to be my mentor, my patient teacher, and my very special friend.

INTRODUCTION

The largest creatures ever to walk this earth were dinosaurs. Where did they come from? When were they here? Why are they not around anymore? These are only a few of the questions that baffle young and old people alike. But where do we find the answers to these questions?

Two theories — creation and evolution — attempt to solve these mysteries, but these two theories are diametrically opposed to each other. For years my husband, Dr. John C. Whitcomb, has lectured on Bible and science issues, coming down strong with "thus saith the Lord." At the end of his lectures it is not uncommon for parents to ask us where they can find Biblical science books on a child's level. Parents are desperate to find something to refute the evolutionary presuppositions presented in their childrens' secular textbooks.

Until the early 1980's, few resources existed that dealt with scientific issues on a child's level. Saddened by this tragic situation, I decided to prepare an illustrated lecture for children using transparencies. This Biblical and scientific presentation so fascinated children that their parents and teachers encouraged me to put it into written form.

That is why this book has been written. However, while children should know facts about dinosaurs, it is more important that they know about themselves — how they got here, why they are here, and where they are going. It is infinitely more important that they not only know God, Who is the Creator of this great Universe and all that is in it, but that they know His Son Jesus Christ as their personal Saviour and Lord.

Throughout my talks with children, and hence throughout this book, I have emphasized the truth of the Gospel. Many children have made decisions to ask Jesus to be their Saviour at the conclusion of my talks. My prayer is that this book will have the same result of leading children of all ages to Christ.

While it is assumed that a great deal is known about dinosaurs, scientists frankly admit that little is known about them. There are only about thirty scientists in the world who are seriously researching dinosaurs. Most of our impressions about dinosaurs come from artist's pictures, which upon further investigation had to be corrected. As more and more fossils are unearthed scientists change their minds. In contrast, God's Word needs no revision. While I have attempted to present current theories, it is my pleasurable responsibility to present Biblical truth that is reliable and never changes.

FOREWORD

In a world of constantly shifting theories, thank God for His sure Word!

The Bible does not claim to be a textbook on science, but God does promise us that His Word contains everything we need to know for "life and godliness" (2 Peter 1:3). When philosophers ask the "big questions" (Why are we? Where did we come from? Where are we going?), they are treading on theological turf!

Students of the Bible and lovers of God cannot afford to surrender the discussion of life origins to "hard science." These questions (and the answers!) are theological by nature. Only someone who was "there" when the universe came into existence can explain how it happened!

Norma Whitcomb has produced this delightful book from a Creationist perspective to excite young, enquiring minds with the splendors of God's original creation. The record in the bones, far from embarrassing Creationists, provides a unique opportunity to impress children with the power of God and also the death and destruction produced by man's sin.

Children have a natural fascination with "those terrible lizards." Through this book, they will also have a divine encounter with the creative intelligence that spoke these creatures into existence.

Jack Wyrtzen
Founder of Word of Life International

Part One

INTRODUCTION TO DINOSAURS

"All things came into being by [Jesus Christ the Word], and apart from Him nothing came into being that has come into being."

JOHN 1:3

Chapter 1

Dinosaurs Are Part of God's Creation

Have you ever stood in a museum looking at the skeleton of a giant dinosaur and wondered where dinosaurs came from? When did they roam the earth? And why are they not around anymore?

About ten thousand years ago, God created this wonderful world for us to explore and enjoy. He was here when everything happened. Then He wrote a book, the Bible, to tell us all about it. The Bible says, "In six days the Lord made the heavens and the earth, the sea and ALL that is in them" (Exodus 20:11). The miraculous way in which God created everything out of nothing, including dinosaurs, in just six days shows how mighty and powerful He really is.

The Bible — the only completely reliable book ever written about God and His world — will be our source as we study about God's creation of all things. God's Word is truth. It is the final authority on what we know about dinosaurs, about ourselves, and about everything else in the world. The contributions of scientists have been invaluable in helping us understand our world. But when scientists study old bones and fossils, they can only make guesses. Their ideas and beliefs change all the time as they make new findings. We appreciate their hard work, but we must not believe their theories if those theories do not agree with what God's Word teaches.

You might be surprised to learn that the Bible tells us some important things about dinosaurs! In the oldest book of the Bible, the book of Job, God told Job to go to the Jordan River and look at Behemoth which He had created (Job 40:15, 23). Creation scientists believe that Behemoth, which is described as a strong, muscular animal, was the largest land dinosaur ever created.

Behemoth - the largest land animal that ever lived!

4

The Bible has more to tell us about dinosaurs. Genesis tells when and how dinosaurs were created. Genesis also tells us that dinosaurs went into the Ark with Noah and his family, lived in

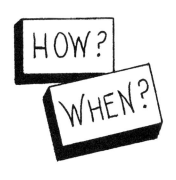

that huge barge for more than a year, and came out with the other animals when the Flood ended.

No land animals alive today are as big as the mighty dinosaur. However, not all dinosaurs were huge. Some were as small as rabbits or even as tiny as little chickens. Fossils of bone structures have given us those facts, but some things still remain a mystery. For instance, we know very little about the skin color of dinosaurs. They might have had stripes, patches or spots. If you had never seen a zebra, you would not know by looking at its skeleton that it had beautiful, symmetrical black-and-white stripes. Likewise, it is impossible to know what the dinosaurs' skin looked like. It is very possible that some had colorful patterns on their skins.

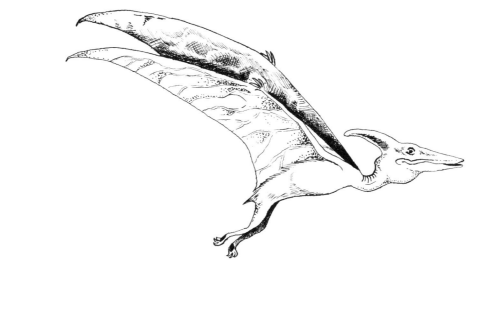

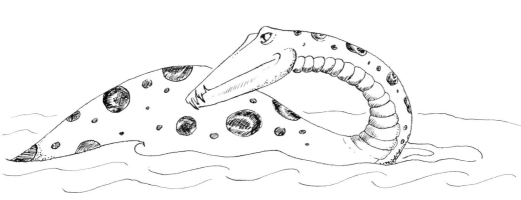

Dinosaurs had other interesting characteristics. They came in many different shapes. Some were skinny and some looked like ostriches. A few were built like armored tanks. Others had unusually long necks and long tails. There were sharp-horned dinosaurs and others with mouths like ducks.

Some dinosaurs could fly while others could swim. Some dinosaurs ate only plants, while others ate meat.

Whether they were meat-eaters or plant-eaters, large or small, swimmers or flyers, all dinosaurs were alike in one way: they had the skeletal structure of a creeping thing. They belonged to the animal family known as **reptiles**.

Thousands of reptiles still live in the world today. Snakes, crocodiles and lizards are all reptiles. Reptiles are cold-blooded animals that depend partly on the temperature of the environment for their body heat. An alligator's temperature might be 80 degrees in the shade, or 92 degrees if it were basking in the sun. Unlike an alligator, you and I are warm-blooded. God has built systems into our body so that our temperature stays almost the same, whatever the temperature of the air around us.

All reptiles that have been discovered to date hatched from eggs. Mother dinosaurs laid their eggs in holes that they dug in the sand. Then they covered the nests with more sand or decaying leaves. Reptiles do not sit on their eggs the way hens do. They rely on the warmth of the sun on the sand to hatch the eggs. When the baby dinosaurs broke through their shells, they would begin darting around on the sand.

Each kind of animal has certain characteristics that make it different from others. Cats come in all sizes — from the fearsome Siberian tiger to the gentle house cat. Yet we know them all as cats by their skeletal structures, the shape and arrangement of their teeth, their padded feet with special claws, and their supple bodies. So, too, we know dinosaurs by their bone structure which is different from other animals. We also know that everything, including dinosaurs, was part of God's original design of a perfect world.

"Dinosaurs are part of God's original design"

"Through [His Son] He made the world."

HEBREWS 1:2

Chapter 2

How Dinosaurs Got Their Names

Have you ever wondered why those mysterious beasts are called "dinosaurs"? About 150 years ago, a group of bone hunters brought some bone fossils to a British scientist named Sir Richard Owen, who studied the structures of bones. He concluded

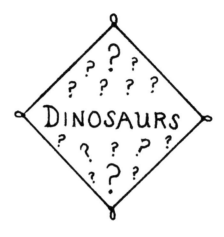

that these strange bones were those of a reptile. But what kind of reptile? He had never seen such huge bones before, so he invented a new word, **dinosauria**, which means "terrible lizard" in Greek. The name was later shortened to "dinosaur."

How did Diplodocus and Triceratops and all the other dinosaurs get their names? Scientists have strict rules for naming plants and animals. The name must describe something special about the plant or animal, and it must be a combination of Greek or Latin words. For example, the name Triceratops (try-SAIR-a-tops) comes from Greek words meaning "three horn face." Can you think of a better

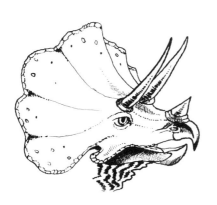

name for a dinosaur with three horns on his face? Deinocheirus (dine-oh-KIRE-us) means "terrible hand." He got that name because he had 12-inch claws in his huge hands.

Why couldn't Triceratops simply be called "Three Horn Face"? Why did his name have to be in Greek or Latin? The answer is that Greek and Latin are very old languages that can be understood by scientists all over the world. "Triceratops" means the same thing in English, German, Russian, or any other language.

Sometimes a dinosaur is named after the person who found the bones. The Yaleosaurus (Yale-ee-oh-SAUR-us) was discovered by Yale University scientists. Other times a dinosaur is named after the place where its bones were discovered, such as the Alamosaurus (Al-a-moh-SAUR-us), whose bones were found in the Alamo Mountains of New Mexico.

Adam was the first person to give names to birds and beasts. He was the most intelligent man ever created by the Almighty God. He never went to school, or studied a textbook, yet he was able to look at each creature God had made and give that creature a unique name. The Bible says, "And out of the ground the Lord God formed every beast of the field and every bird of the sky, and brought them to the Man [Adam] to see what he would call them; and whatever the Man called a living creature, that was its name" (Genesis 2:19). That meant that Adam had to make up names for at least 8,600 birds and 5,500 mammals. Notice that the Bible only mentions birds and mammals. The Bible does not tell us that he named any of the creeping things, so evidently he did not name dinosaurs, insects or marine creatures.

 Adam did something that no other man has ever done. He had such super intelligence that he could remember each animal he had called by name! Why do we not use the names Adam made up for these animals today? Because we do not know the language that Adam spoke. It was lost at the Tower of Babel judgment (Genesis 11:7-9).

Even though we call them "terrible lizards" today, God did not create dinosaurs as terrible creatures. Genesis 1:31 says that "God saw everything that He had made, and behold it was very good." Animals did not harm or kill each other until Adam sinned. God had them and all of His creation under His perfect control.

"In the beginning God created the heavens and the earth."

Genesis 1:1

Chapter 3

Differences Between Men and Animals

Your great-great-great-great-grandfather probably never heard of dinosaurs. About one hundred and fifty years ago, a wave of excitement swept around the world when the first bones and fossils of dinosaurs were discovered and people began to realize that giant creeping things once roamed this beautiful planet.

Dinosaurs definitely lived on our earth — there is nothing make-believe about these mysterious creatures. But what about "ape-men" and "cave men"? Did they really exist?

Many books, including many science books, show drawings of ape-men. They are usually pictured with ape-like teeth, long arms, and lots of hair covering their bodies. These drawings are not like the drawings of dinosaurs, which were reconstructed from fossilized bones. These drawings of ape-men are completely from the artists' imaginations — they never saw such a man, or his bones, because such a man never existed. The idea is as false as a "zebra-man" or an "armadillo-man."

The ape-man idea is not a harmless imaginary thing to play with. Why? Because it denies what the Bible says about Man. God's Word says that Man was made in the likeness of God. The Bible never talks about a half-animal/half-man. Neither is there anything in science to show that such a creature ever lived.

The physical differences between men and animals are great. But the spiritual and mental differences are even greater. An animal cannot read or select words and put them into meaningful sentences. Only Man can do that. Man

makes choices, whereas an animal is controlled by instinct. An animal cannot think about the past or the future, or even about itself. Only Man can know where he came from, why he is here, and where he is going. Only Man can feel guilty when he does wrong, because only Man has a conscience. Man can know who God is, and what He has done. Only Man can worship God as His Creator.

Ape-men have never existed, but there have been many "cave men." They did not look or act like those in the comic strips. They were not savage people who acted like animals. Some, like David, were intelligent people who lived in caves because cruel men forced them to do so. The Bible says that David was a man after God's own heart (I Samuel 13:14). King Saul was chasing him and his followers, so they hid in caves for protection (I Samuel 22-24). It was while David was a "cave man" that he composed two of his great psalms (Psalms 57, 142; cf. Hebrews 11:38).

The Bible tells us about a time in the future when nearly everyone will live in caves. "And the kings of the earth and the great men and the commanders and the rich and the strong and every slave and free man [will hide] themselves in the caves and among the rocks of the mountains" (Revelation 6:15; cf. Isaiah 2:19-22). Why? Because they will be afraid of God, whose salvation they have rejected.

Ape-men only exist in the imaginations of people who do not know God's truth about creation. But cave-men were real people who had God's image and likeness. Men were never animals. They were directly created by God as distinctly separate creatures. Between Man and animals there lies a great gap that can never be bridged.

Men will hide in caves.

Chapter 4

Fossils

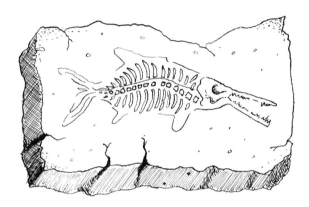

Billions of fossils have been found in every continent of the world. Fossils are traces of plants, marine creatures or land animals that were buried suddenly under mud, sand or lava. The mud then hardened before the plants and animals decomposed, thereby preserving an imprint. Most of the fossils we find today were made at the time of the great Flood.

Dinosaurs began to die out after the Flood, about six thousand years ago. The first dinosaur bones were discovered in 1822 by an English woman named Mary Ann Mantell. The bones sparked the interest of her husband, Dr. Gideon

Dinosaurs became extinct about 6,000 years ago.

Mantell, who was an avid amateur fossil hunter. As he began to find more dinosaur bones, people became excited and inquisitive. About thirty years later there was a dinosaur bone rush as scientists from America and Europe frantically competed to uncover fossils and bones.

Thousands of dinosaur fossils and bones were found, including whole skeletons.

The bones were carefully dug from the ground, wrapped and labeled. Then they were sent to museums where scientists could spend a lot of time studying the bones, teeth and footprints of these mysterious creatures. A scientist who studies fossils is called a paleontologist (pay-lee-un-TALL-uh-jist).

Each new discovery reveals more about what dinosaurs were like. A paleontologist may be able to know what type of food a dinosaur ate by studying a fossil tooth. Footprints preserved in rock can show how a dinosaur walked. The size and shape of a bone may give a clue to the size of the muscle that was attached to it.

20

You, too, can study an animal's skeleton. The next time you eat chicken for dinner, look at how the meat is attached to the leg bones. Collect all the chicken bones and try to fit them together into a proper skeleton.

Now imagine what it would be like putting together the skeleton of a huge dinosaur! It requires time, patience and skill for a scientist to put a dinosaur skeleton together. To do so, he compares the bones with those of other reptiles. He also studies the fossils of other animals. By doing this, the scientist has an idea of what the dinosaur looked like.

When animals die today, they generally do not become fossils. Why? Because most animals fall to the ground and are picked to pieces by scavengers, such as hawks or other meat-eating animals. Fish are eaten by scavenger fish before they ever hit bottom. Plants are not preserved either. They wither and crumble. In order to become a fossil, plants and animals must be pressed under a great weight of mud and instantly preserved.

The billions of fossils give us scientific clues, and they give us a warning as well. The Bible says, "through one man sin entered into the world" (Romans 5:12). Because of man's sin, "the Lord was sorry that He  had made man on the earth" (Genesis 6:6), and so he sent the great Flood to "blot out man . . . from the face of the land, from man to animals to creeping things and to birds of the sky" (Genesis 6:7). The fossils of smothered, drowned, mangled and smashed animals remind us of the message in God's Word that says, "The wages of sin is DEATH" (Romans 6:23). But the resurrection of Jesus Christ after His death on the Cross offers eternal life to all who believe in Him.

Part Two

DIFFERENT DINOSAUR TYPES

*"By [Jesus Christ] all things were created,
both in the heavens and on earth,
visible and invisible."*

COLOSSIANS 1:16

Chapter 5

The Giant Reptiles

DIPLODOCUS

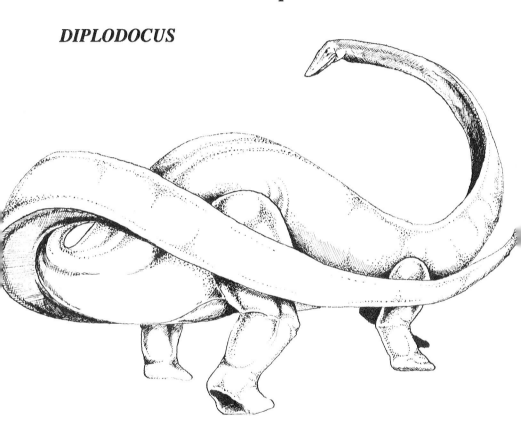

Diplodocus (dip-lo-DOC-us) was one of the longest dinosaurs that ever prowled our earth. He was about 100 feet long. That is longer than seven big cars lined up waiting for the light to turn green! His name means "double beam," because his neck and his tail resemble huge beams sticking out of each end of his body. With such a long neck in front, he needed an equally long tail behind to keep his body balanced, like a see-saw. His neck was so long that he could have looked at you through the window on the fourth floor of a building.

For Diplodocus, every day was an all-day feast. He could weave his long, graceful neck in and out of the treetops, or he could drop it down to eat plants on the floor of the forest. His teeth were shaped like short pencil stubs. Because his teeth were not very strong, perhaps he could take only small bites of soft water plants. Diplodocus had to spend most of his time eating hundreds of pounds of plants to feed his huge body.

Diplodocus had a hole on the very top of his skull. Perhaps he breathed through this hole. If so, he could walk along the bottom of a deep lake, and still breathe easily with just the top of his head poking out of the water. Many of these dinosaurs splashed through the lakes and marshes of what is now the western part of the United States.

BRONTOSAURUS
(APATOSAURUS)

Brontosaurus (bront-oh-SAWR-us), recently renamed Apatosaurus (uh-pat-oh-SAWR-us), was not as long as Diplodocus, but he was much heavier. He weighed as much as 40 tons, which is 80,000 pounds! Eight elephants put together would equal one Brontosaurus. Because he was so heavy, scientists thought that when he walked, he must have made a noise like thunder, so they named him "thunder lizard" (bronto = "thunder" and saurus = "lizard").

A man standing on the shoulders of another man could barely reach the shoulders of a Brontosaurus. His 30-foot-long tail must have made him look as though he were dragging a tree behind him. His 20-foot-long neck put his head high in the trees where he could easily eat all the leaves that he needed. His 75-foot-long body made him almost as long as two school buses parked end-to-end!

God equipped Brontosaurus with thick, straight legs full of muscle to hold up all that weight. Each leg ended with a padded foot in which were buried five stubby toes. This gentle giant made a footprint big enough for a child to sit in.

Actually, Brontosaurus never really existed! A paleontologist discovered the bones of his body, but the head was missing, so he added the head of another dinosaur which he found a few miles away. Since then, Brontosaurus has been reassembled with the right head and renamed Apatosaurus.

Apatosaurus was an herbivore, which means that he ate only plants. He had 24 spoon-shaped teeth that were not very good for chewing food, so he solved this problem by swallowing rough stones about the size of a man's fist. These stones helped grind up the food in his gizzard. Birds and crocodiles do that, too.

It is believed that Apatosaurus, as well as some other dinosaurs, lived and traveled in family groups. They protected the young ones by keeping them in the middle of the herd.

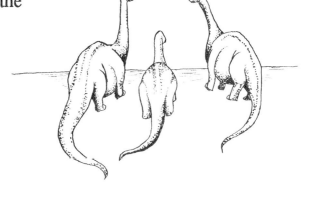

Apatosaurus probably waded into deep water to get food and to protect himself from dreadful flesh-eating reptiles. Another reason he may have preferred the water is because of his massive weight. Have you ever been in a lake or pool and held another person in your arms? Remember how light he felt? Being in water helped Apatosaurus feel lighter too, thereby taking some of the weight off his legs.

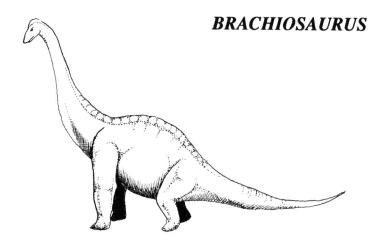

BRACHIOSAURUS

Apatosaurus was an enormous dinosaur, but Brachiosaurus (brack-ee-oh-SAWR-us) was much bigger. His weight of 80 tons made him twice as large as Apatosaurus. He was 50 feet high; it would have been easy for him to look into the window on the fifth floor of a building.

The nostril of the Brachiosaurus was in a strange place — on top of his head! Having his nostril there may have enabled him to hide from his enemies under water, but raise his head just high enough out of the water (sort of like a periscope on a submarine) to breathe.

ULTRASAURUS

For a long time Brachiosaurus was called "the biggest of the big," until the bones of the Ultrasaurus (ul-truh-SAWR-us) were found. The Ultrasaurus was about 100 feet long and weighed about 200,000 pounds. That would be about the weight of 6,000 of your friends put together!

'ULTRASAURUS 200,000 Pounds -- WOW!"

SIESMOSAURUS

Recently, even bigger bones have been found! They belong to the Siesmosaurus (size-mow-SAWR-us), or "earth shaker." He is called that because his stupendous size and weight must have made the ground tremble as he put down one heavy foot after another. As far as we know, the Siesmosaurus discovered in 1985 is the biggest dinosaur that ever lived—although he may be simply a larger version of the famous Brachiosaurus.

TYRANNOSAURUS REX

The mighty Tyrannosaurus Rex (Tuh-ran-uh-SAWR-us Rex) was probably the greatest and most terrible killing machine that ever walked the earth. Tyranno means "tyrant," saurus means "lizard," and Rex means "king." Thus, Tyrannosaurus Rex means "King of tyrant lizards." Certainly, every man and animal on the earth was afraid of him.

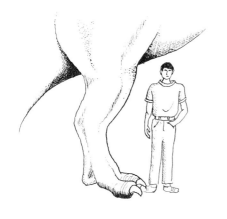

This "king of tyrant lizards" was fifteen feet tall when standing upright on his hind legs. A tall man standing next to Tyrannosaurus Rex would just reach his knee.

His hind feet were equipped with enormous claws. Each foot covered more than seven square feet. That is as large as a huge truck tire. He had such a big stride that he could cross an average room in one step. His back legs were strong and heavy, but his front legs were small and stunted.

His head was about six feet long — as long as an average-sized table. His eye sockets were so large that a man could put his head through them. Scientists have classified Tyrannosaurus Rex as a carnivore, which means that he ate meat. He had 60 six-inch-long teeth in his huge head that were like daggers with jagged edges, like a steak knife, which made it easy for him to slice through meat. However, recent findings lead us to believe that he may have eaten soft foods as well.

Teeth as long
as bananas

If this monster lost a tooth, he would grow another to take its place. We are told that if he lost a tooth fifty times, a new one grew back each time. Sharks have this amazing ability as well. A shark has rows of teeth underneath each other, so he can replace ones that fall out. That is why we find so many sharks' teeth on the beaches.

Tyrannosaurus Rex had a jaw so big, he could have swallowed you whole. In fact, he could swallow more meat in one mouthful than four human beings could eat in a month. His stomach was so huge that he could eat enough at one time to wait a week or more between meals. Scientists have calculated that this beast ate more than 40 tons of meat a year!

"40 tons of meat in 1 year!"

Chapter 6

The Unusual Dinosaurs

TRICERATOPS

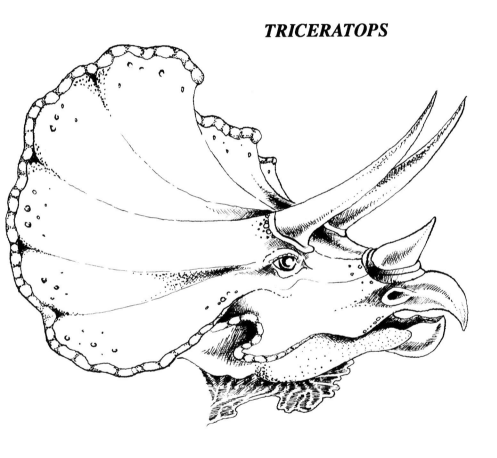

God created some scary dinosaurs, but He also created some funny-looking ones. One of them was the ten-ton monster known as Triceratops (try-SAIR-uh-tops), which means "three horn face." Triceratops would never have won a beauty contest, but he might have won an eating contest! He had powerful jaws and grinding teeth that could smash up the toughest plants. Even though Triceratops was an herbivore, scientists believe that he was a mighty fighter.

In fact, Triceratops looked like a big army tank with three machine guns coming out of his head. Two 24-inch horns stuck out above his eyes and a shorter horn stuck out above his eagle-like beak. As long as he could face his enemies, he could fight them off with his strong, pointed horns. Perhaps the six-inch-thick bony shield that went half-way around his neck also protected him from meat-eating enemies. Nearly one-third of his body was his gigantic head, which was seven feet long and as high as a basketball hoop. He needed a neck chock full of muscles to hold up such a big head.

Another funny-looking dinosaur was Stegasaurus (steg-uh-SAWR-us). He looked as if he had sails sticking straight out of his back, all the way from his head to his tail. This single row of bony plates may have regulated his body temperature by expelling heat when he was too warm, and absorbing heat when he was too cold.

Stegasaurus means "curved lizard," because he had strongly curved ribs. At the end of his tail he had four spikes that were three feet long and  nearly six inches thick. Perhaps he whipped his tail around to pierce the tough hides of his enemies.

Stegasaurus had a three-ounce brain no larger than a walnut, but his body weighed seven to ten tons. That is like putting the brain of a kitten into the head of a full-grown elephant. The description of "all brawn and no brain" fits Stegasaurus very well.

Stegasaurus had a bone at the base of his spine with a cavity twenty times bigger than his brain. It is thought that this hole contained a nerve center that functioned like a second brain to control the movement of his tail and hind legs. So every time he had a thought, he must have had an after-thought!

PACHYCEPHALOSAURUS

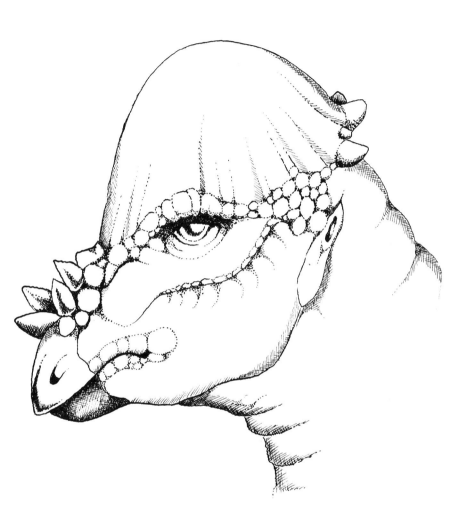

Without a doubt, the ugliest dinosaur of all was Pachycephalosaurus (pack-ee-sef-uh-luh-SAWR-us). His name means "thick-headed lizard," but he is called "bonehead" by many. His ugliness did not make him fierce, however. Most likely he was a gentle plant-eating reptile.

Pachycephalosaurus was about six feet tall — about the height of a man. His skull was about two feet long, with wart-like, bony knobs over most of it. To make him look even more ugly, he had several bony spikes on his nose. On the top of his domed skull was a very thick, six- to ten-inch mass. No one knows why God put it there. Perhaps the reptile used it as a means of defense by butting other animals. It seems unlikely that he needed it to protect his very small brain.

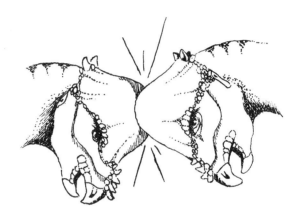

Can you imagine a dinosaur that looked like a duck? Some dinosaurs had mouths the shape of a duck's bill. These are called duck-billed dinosaurs. While not all duck-billed dinosaurs looked alike, they were all slow-moving plant-eaters.

Some duckbills had two rows of teeth at the back of their upper jaw, and two rows of teeth at the back of their lower jaw. Each row had as many as 500 teeth. That is 2,000 teeth in one mouth! These teeth were not all used at the same time, however. One row of teeth was hidden underneath the top row. They were held in reserve to replace teeth that fell out, just like the teeth of the Tyrannosaurus Rex.

One of the strangest things about duckbills was their heads. Some were flat-headed, while others had peculiar horn-shaped or boney crests on top of their heads. Inside the crests and horns were twisted tubes connected to their windpipes and nostrils. Perhaps they stored air in these tubes so they could stay under water longer. God designed the duckbills' crests as a means of protection. These tubes may have given the duckbills a keen sense of smell for detecting enemies, or have served as a trumpet for making a loud noise to scare predators.

In 1908, a fossil collector found remains of two duckbills in Wyoming. Even the skins were preserved, so scientists know more about what some duckbills looked like. They had thick, leathery  skin, like the skin of crocodiles. It appears that they had dark backs and light colored bellies. Recently, a whole graveyard of duckbills was found in northern Alaska.

Trachadon

The most common duckbilled dinosaur was the 18-foot-tall Trachadon (TRAK-uh-don), which means "rough tooth." His coarse teeth were well-suited for grinding the tough vegetation that this reptile probably liked to eat.

Corythosaurus

One crested duck-billed dinosaur was known as Corythosaurus (kuh-rith-uh-SAWR-us), the "helmet lizard." On top of his head was a bony mass in the shape of a semi-circle that looked like a helmet.

Parasaurolophus

Parasaurolophus (pair-uh-sawr-uh-LOFF-us) was known as the "crest lizard." He had a hollow, curved tube that stretched out straight behind his head like a stiff ponytail. This tube formed an extremely long passage to his nose and might have been used to make a sound like a trombone. Can you imagine

the hooting that a bunch of "trombone heads" would have made when they got together?!

Lambeosaurus

Another duckbill is the Lambeosaurus (lam-bee-oh-SAWR-us), which was named after a famous geologist, Lawrence Lambe. The crest on top of this reptile's head was shaped like a top hat.

For a long time, scientists thought the duckbills used their shovel-shaped mouths to scoop up food from the bottom of swamps. Then a German scientist discovered some plants inside a duckbill's skeleton that were the dinosaur's last meal before he was instantly destroyed by the Flood and fossilized. The plants were hard, pine tree needles. Clues like this, as well as his rough teeth, would seem to indicate that he ate tough things from the shores of swamps and rivers, as opposed to soft foods from under the water.

MYSTERY

The duckbills are still an unsolved mystery. We are not sure about their eating habits, or whether they lived on land or in swamps. Other questions remain, such as how they used the webs on their feet or the crests on their heads. Maybe someday scientists will be able to tell us more about these fascinating creatures. But in the meantime we can be sure of one thing: the Bible makes it clear that duckbilled dinosaurs, as well as all the other land-dwelling dinosaurs, were created by God on the final day of His wonderful creation week — the same day He created mankind.

"God. . . calls into being that which does not exist."

ROMANS 4:17

Chapter 7

Reptiles of the Sea

The Bible says, "And God created the great sea monsters" (Genesis 1:21). God described one of these creatures to Job. He called the creature Leviathan (Job 41:1). Some people think God is describing a crocodile, but the description does not fit. The Bible says, "Lay your hand on him; remember the battle; you will not do it again!" (Job 41:8).

People could not catch him with hooks, and he was so strong they could not hurt him with spears or swords (Job 41:1-2). We do not know which sea monster was described, but God said that "nothing on earth is like him, one made without fear" (Job 41:33).

"And God created sea monsters"

It seems almost impossible that a creature could shoot flames out of its mouth, but the Bible says that "out of his [Leviathan's] mouth go burning torches; sparks of fire leap forth" (Job 41:19). This verse gives us another reason we know that this mighty creature could not have been a crocodile. We do not see crocodiles or any other reptile today that can shoot fire from its mouth. However, God has preserved little, half-inch beetles that show us how shooting "fire" could have been possible. These are the Bombardier Beetles, which got their names from a special little cannon in their tails.

These beetles are the first poison gas specialists. They have a defense system like tear gas and a tommy gun all in one. In their tails are two chambers with a special gas in each. When they sense danger, they mix these two gases. The gases shoot through two rotating nozzles at the rear of their bodies, mix just outside those nozzles, and explode. The ball of hot, noxious gas hits their enemy every time.

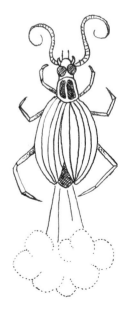

48

ICHTHYOSAURUS

The first marine reptile fossils ever discovered were found in England by an eleven-year-old girl named Mary Anning. She hunted and sold fossil shells to support herself

and her widowed mother. In 1910, she and her brother saw some bones sticking out of a cliff. With a hammer and chisel, Mary chipped away at the rock until she traced the outline of a whole skeleton. The creature had four flippers and long jaws full of sharp teeth, and it looked like

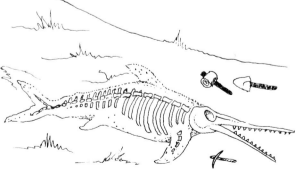

both a reptile and a fish. Mary had found the first, almost complete skeleton of an extinct marine reptile! This creature came to be known as Ichthyosaurus (ick-thee-oh-SAWR-us). This name comes from the two Greek words for "fish" and "lizard."

The streamlined body of Ichthyosaurus was very similar to that of the fast-moving porpoises. His head was drawn into a long, thin snout fringed with small, spiked teeth. His two pairs of side paddles probably steered him through the water, while the fins near the base of his tail caused him to swim swiftly. One ichthyosaur reached a length of 30 feet, and another (Opthalmosaurus) appeared not to have any teeth.

PLESIOSAURUS

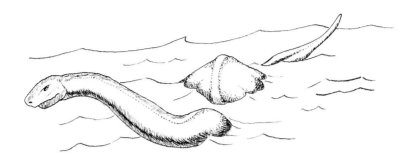

A few years later, Mary Anning discovered the bones of another seagoing reptile, Plesiosaurus (plaz-ee-oh-SAWR-us). Plesiosaurs was less fish-like in appearance than Ichthyosaurus. Some plesiosaurs had extremely long necks and relatively small heads with sharply pointed teeth. Their tails were short and pointed. One variety of short-necked plesiosaurs looked somewhat like the killer whales of today. Another variety must have moved through the water like a big machine, eating everything in sight. His eight-foot-long head made it possible for him to eat creatures as big as giant sea turtles.

In 1925, Charles Moore was walking along Moore's Beach, two miles north of Santa Cruz, California. He came upon the decaying carcass of a serpent-like monster that had washed ashore. People came from near and far to take pictures of the creature. The Santa Cruz News said that the

beast "was observed to have a head bigger than a barrel, eyes bigger than an abalone and an oval-shaped body." Another witness described "two short feet as flippers," and suggested that it "probably swam with its head high above the water." If they were right, this could have been a variety of plesiosaur.

God created some awesome marine creatures that display his creative power. Evolutionists say that living creatures started from a speck in the ocean that after billions of years evolved into all kinds of water and land animals. They say that some land mammals later went back into the ocean and then slowly evolved into water mammals. However, no one has ever found a fossil that is half-way between a land mammal and a sea mammal.

The most important reason we know that these scientists are wrong is because the Bible says that God created all the sea creatures. They did not evolve from something else. They were created by God just as they are as a sign of His great power.

"Sea creatures did not evolve"

Chapter 8

Reptiles of the Air

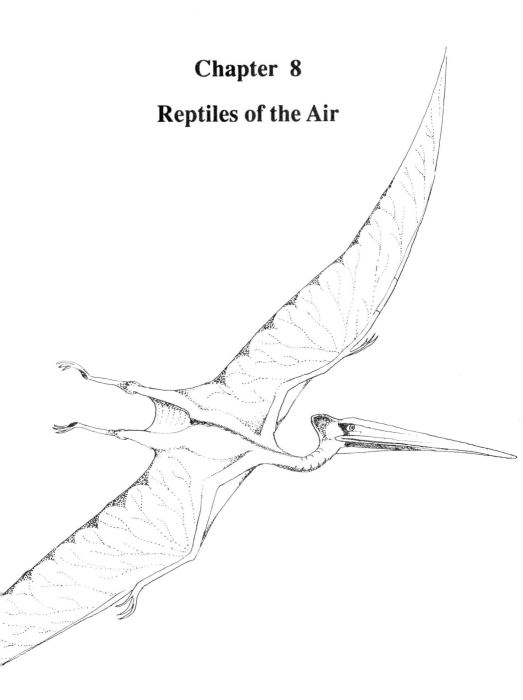

God created reptiles that swam in the water. He also created reptiles that flew in the air. It is believed that some flying reptiles grew to be as big as sailboats! Their Creator God constructed their ultralight forms so that they could spread their wings and lift off in a gentle breeze and fly away!

PTERANADON

Pteranadon (ter-AN-uh-don) was a flying reptile with a 50-foot wingspread. He had a six-foot-long head, including a crest that stuck out 27 inches behind. This crest, which in some places was as thin as four sheets of paper, acted as an aerodynamic balance to his long toothless beak.

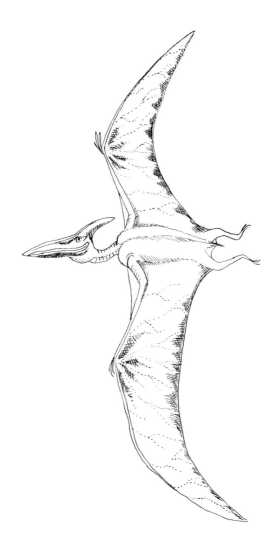

Even though he was large in size, he weighed only about 26 pounds! God designed this magnificent creature for flight. His hollow bones made him lightweight and more efficient than a modern glider.

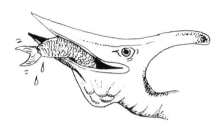

Under his throat, the Pteranadon had a pouch in which to store small fish and marine animals that he plucked from the water. Perhaps he was light colored, to help him blend with the sky so that he would not scare the surface fish which were probably his main diet.

Fossils of the Pteranadon were first discovered in the 1860's and more continue to be found in Nebraska, Kansas and Texas.

ARCHAEOPTERYX

Archaeopteryx (AR-kee-OP-ter-riks) was a winged creature with feathers. His name means "ancient wing." He had claws on his wings, making him able to climb trees as well as fly. However, the claws are not an evidence that this creature was evolving from a reptile into a bird. No skeleton has ever been found that shows any "in-between" (evolutionary) stages.

Even today, in South America, there is a bird called a HOATZIN that both flies and climbs trees. He has two claws on the first two fingers of each wing, but he is obviously not evolving into a bird.

RHAMPHORHYNCHUS

Rhamphorhynchus (ram-for-HINK-us) was one of the smaller flying reptiles, about one-and-a-half feet long. He was one of the oddest looking flying reptiles because of his long, skinny tail that had a rudder at the end.

These reptiles would not be able to fly in our world today, because there has been a drastic change in the earth's atmosphere. This change happened at the time of the Great Flood. We will read more about those changes in chapter 17.

"By faith we understand that the worlds were prepared by the word of God, so that what is seen was not made out of things which are visible"

HEBREWS 11:3

Part Three

DINOSAURS BEFORE THE FLOOD

"There is. . . one Lord, Jesus Christ, by whom are all things, and we exist through Him."

1 CORINTHIANS 8:6

Chapter 9

Dinosaurs and Men Lived at the Same Time

The Bible tells us that dinosaurs and men co-existed (lived together at the same time). God said to Job, "Behold ... Behemoth, which I made as well as you" (Job 40:15-17). God told Job that Behemoth had unusually powerful muscles and bones as strong as iron, and that he was a grass-eater. Some people think this describes an elephant or a hippopotamus. A clue in verse 17 proves this is not so. The Bible says that "He [Behemoth] bends his tail like a cedar tree." Does an elephant look as though he is dragging a tall cedar tree behind him? Is the tail of a hippopotamus as big around as a cedar tree? Not at all. Creation scientists believe that God

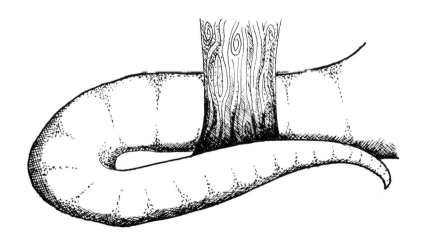

was describing a dinosaur. Perhaps Job saw the biggest land animal that ever lived. The Bible says that, "He is the first of the ways of God" (Job 40:19). This does not mean that this fearless creature was the first one ever to be created. It means that there was nothing as awesome as this gigantic monster.

God told Job to go to the Jordan River to see this mysterious creature. He said, "If a river rages, he is not alarmed" (Job 40:23). In spring, the snow in the mountains of Lebanon, about 50 miles north of the Jordan River, melts. The water rushes down into the peaceful Jordan River, making it a raging torrent. This roaring mass of water did not scare the long-necked

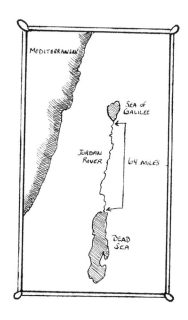

dinosaur. The Bible says, "he is confident, though the Jordan rushes to his mouth" (Job 40:23). The Behemoth just raised his head higher and higher to eat the plants as they floated by. God told Job to "behold," or watch this huge creature. The dinosaur must have been living if God told Job to go look at it.

"He is confident though the Jordan rushes to his mouth."

Evolutionists tell us that dinosaurs lived on this earth from 65 to 200 million years ago. They say that these beasts died out at the end of the Mesozoic Era, which is their name for the dinosaur age. According to their theory, dinosaurs died out millions of years before man lived on this planet. They have formed this theory without considering God's Book. But those who carefully study the Bible, as well as facts of science, agree that this evolutionary theory is not true.

No evolutionist was living when dinosaurs were here. The only way anyone can be sure what happened at that time is to check it out with somebody who was there. God is the Creator of everything. He was there when creation happened! He wrote a book, the Bible, to tell us what He did and how He did it. According to His Book, people, dinosaurs and all other animals lived on this earth at the same time.

Chapter 10

When Were Dinosaurs Created?

In Genesis chapter one, God tells us that He created the entire world in six days. At the beginning of the first day there was only darkness and a formless, watery earth. Then God created light, and "there was evening and there was morning, one day" (Genesis 1:5). On the second day, God separated the waters to make a canopy above the earth. On day three, He formed the dry land and the seas upon the earth. The world was beginning to take form. Then He created full-grown trees, grass, bushes and all other kinds of vegetation on the earth. On the fourth day God made the sun, the moon and the stars to give light to the earth and to mark the days and the seasons.

On the fifth day God began to populate the earth with living creatures. The Bible says, "God created the great sea monsters, and every living creature that moves, with which the waters swarmed after their kind" (Gen. 1:21). "Sea monsters" includes the mighty Leviathan mentioned in Job 41 and Psalm 104:26, as well as whales and great fishes. Gen. 1:21 tells us that "every winged bird after its kind" was created on the fifth day also.

On the sixth and final day of creation, "God made the beasts of the earth after their kind, and the cattle after their kind, and everything that creeps on the ground after its kind." Remember that creeping things include dinosaurs. "And God created man in His own image . . . male and female He created them" (Genesis 1:25, 27).

It is hard for many people to believe what God says about His creation of creeping things. They think it took billions of years for animals to evolve from chemicals in the water. God, who knows everything even before it happens, knew that men would not believe Him. That may be why He tells us three times (Genesis 1:24, 25, 26) that He made every creeping thing at the same time that He created man and woman.

God created land dinosaurs including the powerful Behemoth (Job 40:15) on the sixth day of creation. When he made them, they were harmless plant-eaters. The Bible says, " . . . and to every thing that moves on the earth which has life, I have given every green plant for food" (Genesis 1:30). Instead of eating each other, the animals ate plants,

nuts, berries and fruits. It was not until after Adam and Eve sinned that many animals became flesh-eaters.

Before the sin of man, God's entire creation was flawless and complete. Nature was balanced according to God's perfect plan. He had no need to wait for life to evolve, since He made everything exactly the way He wanted it, without any provision for time to make things better. Only an omnipotent (all powerful), mighty God could have created such a perfect world.

"In six days the Lord made the heavens, the earth, the sea and all that is in them."

EXODUS 20:11

Chapter 11

The Vapor Canopy

Our world was very different before the Flood. God had placed a shield of water above the atmosphere all around the earth (Genesis 1:6-8). No, Adam could not see it. Neither could Cain nor Noah nor any of the other people who lived before the Flood. It was a canopy of water vapor, and vapor is an invisible gas. The people could see the sun by day and the moon and stars by night through the canopy.

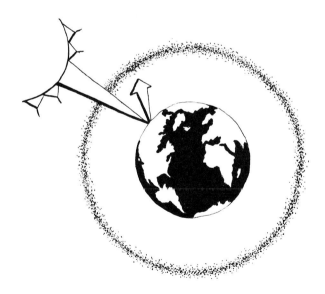

This canopy was part of God's wonderful plan. When God told Noah that rain would come down from above, He meant that the vapor in the canopy would turn into drops of water. Then rain would come down for the very first time.

God's Word describes it this way: "And the floodgates of the sky were opened" (Genesis 7:11). The Flood was caused partially by those water drops that fell in torrents upon the earth.

> **"And the flood gates of the sky were opened."**

The vapor canopy kept the earth's heat from escaping, so there were no cold Arctic or Antarctic regions. The temperature stayed the same all year round, all over the world. The warm, humid climate must have felt much like the big greenhouses that we walk into today.

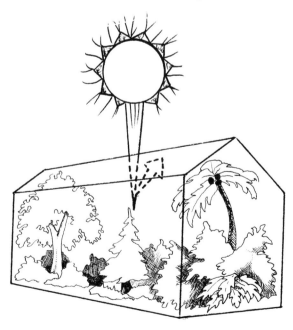

Scientists tell us that the sun's ultraviolet light is deadly to all kinds of life. For 1,600 years the invisible canopy shielded the sun's rays from the earth, so that plants, animals and people lived longer and grew bigger than they do today.

"By the word of the Lord the heavens were made."

PSALM 33:6

Chapter 12

The Wrong Choice

God had prepared a perfect place called the Garden of Eden for Adam and Eve to live in. They would never get sick or die, and they had the freedom to enjoy everything in the Garden. God gave them just one command: not to eat "from the tree of the knowledge of good and evil" (Genesis 2:17). He told them that if they ate from that tree, they would die.

Then something terrible happened in the Garden. Satan tempted Eve through a serpent to eat the fruit from the forbidden tree, and she did. Adam ate the fruit also. Adam and Eve made the wrong choice when they disobeyed God. To disobey God is sin.

God was not pleased with Adam and Eve's sin. He punished them by sending them out of the Garden forever (Genesis 3:23). From then on, Adam would have to work very hard growing grains and vegetables to eat. Hard work

would make him and Eve very tired. Ever since then, people get tired and their bodies get sick. When Adam and Eve sinned, changes took place in the animal kingdom so that some animals, including some dinosaurs, become killers.

God tells us that sin will separate us from Him forever. The Bible says, "your iniquities have made a separation between you and your God, and your sins have hidden His face from you" (Isaiah 59:2). If you live in sin all your life,

you will not go to Heaven when you die.

But there is good news. No one has to stay in that sinful condition. God promises forgiveness for sins, and He tells us what to do to get that forgiveness. He says, "Believe in the Lord Jesus Christ and you shall be saved" (Acts 16:31). Believing that Jesus Christ died on the cross and rose again from the dead will save you from your sin. The Bible says, "For God so loved the world that He gave His only begotten Son, that whoever believes in Him should not perish, but have eternal life" (John 3:16). God has promised, "as many as received Him, to them he gave the right to become children of God, even to those who believe in His name" (John 1:12). Because of Adam and Eve's wrong choice, everybody is born in sin, but each person can choose to accept Jesus as his Savior.

"*Of everything that creeps on the ground, there went into the ark to Noah by twos, male and female, as God had commanded Noah.*"

GENESIS 7:8-9

Part Four

DINOSAURS AND THE GREAT FLOOD

"Of every creeping thing of the ground after its kind, two of every kind shall come to you to keep them alive."

GENESIS 6:20

Chapter 13

Noah Built the Ark

People multiplied upon the earth and so did their wickedness and sin. Finally, God could not stand the evil any longer. Sin grieved God's heart, so He decided to destroy everything that He had made. The Lord said, "I will blot out man whom I have created from the face of the land, from man to animals to creeping things and to birds of the sky; for I am sorry that I have made them" (Genesis 6:7). Because of sin, God planned to send a flood to destroy everything on the earth.

However, God found one man, Noah, who was righteous, because he trusted God. Noah pleased God, so God told him to build an Ark to warn the world of God's judgment. The Ark would also save Noah's family and representatives of all kinds of birds and land animals. God said that He would bring two of every kind of air-breathing animal into the Ark. He told Noah, "Of the birds after their kind, and of the animals after their kind, of every creeping thing of the ground after its kind, two of every kind shall come to you to keep them alive" (Genesis 6:20). He brought seven of each of the clean animals to the Ark, because one of  each of these was to be used for sacrifices when the Flood ended (Genesis 8:20). Since the people could eat only clean animals, the extra animals would also provide food for the people.

It was not necessary for Noah to build fish tanks for piranhas, or killer whales, or other marine creatures. Though most marine creatures were destroyed in the violent flood water, God preserved enough of them to multiply after the catastrophe ended.

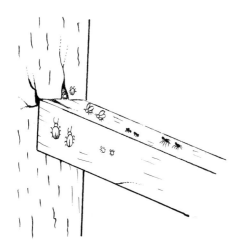

Can you imagine the sight of thousands of insects buzzing and crawling inside the Ark! They probably squeezed into cracks and rested on beams, so Noah did not have to build anything special for them.

God gave Noah careful instructions for building the Ark (Genesis 6:14-16). It was to have three decks with rooms for the animals. Each room, which was probably like a stall, was just right for the needs of the animals in it. This huge barge was built with very strong gopher wood. It was covered inside and out with something called "pitch,"

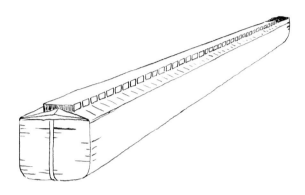

which would keep the wood from rotting and the water from seeping in. The Ark had windows near the top and one door at the side. It had straight sides and a flat bottom, just like the barges that float in the water today.

God even gave Noah the exact size to build the Ark. Your Bible gives the dimensions in the Hebrew word, which is "cubit." A cubit was the length of a man's arm from the tip of his middle finger to his elbow. That is approximately

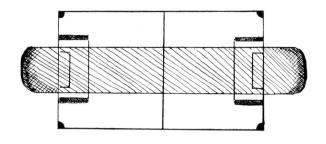

The Ark -- longer than a football field.

eighteen inches. The description in Genesis 6:15 tells us that the Ark was 450 feet long, 75 feet wide and 45 feet high. It was longer than a football field and higher than a three-story building. It was not until 1884 that a ship longer than the Ark was built.

Noah did not have to take a course in navigation to learn how to pilot his barge. The Ark was not going anywhere special. Its purpose was to simply float on the shoreless ocean until the Flood was over.

The Bible says, "for the Lord God had not sent rain upon the earth" (Genesis 2:5). Since it had never rained, it must have been strange for Noah to hear God say that there was going to be a Flood. Noah and God must have had a conversation something like this:

"God, what is rain?"

"Rain is great drops of water that fall from the sky."

"But God, it has never rained."

"It is going to rain, Noah"

"It is going to rain for the first time. Get busy, Noah. Start to build the Ark!"

"What is an Ark, God?"

"The Ark will be a barge to float on the water. Don't fret, I will tell you exactly how to build it."

Noah believed God, obeyed God, and started to build the Ark. But the people were so wicked and unbelieving that they probably made fun of Noah while he and his helpers made logs into boards and hammered them into place to make that spectacular structure. Can you imagine the scene as Noah's neighbors questioned him?

"What are you doing, Noah?"

"I'm building a big barge."

"Why are you doing that?"

Noah answered, "Because water is going to cover the earth and destroy everything that is not in the barge."

They mocked him, saying, "You are crazy, Noah!"

"No, I'm not. I am obeying God. I'm building an Ark to save my family, and the beasts and the birds and the creeping things. If you believe what I am telling you, you can also enter the Ark and be saved."

They kept on mocking him. "Don't you know that it has never rained on the earth before?"

While Noah kept on obeying God and building the Ark, he answered, "I know it. I have not lived 600 years for nothing. I know a lot about what has not yet happened in the world. Do not make fun of what I tell you. Believe what God has said and come into the Ark with me and my family. Come in and be saved from the terrible flood."

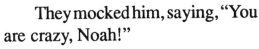

"Believe God and be saved"

It took Noah and his helpers 120 years to build the Ark. That was a long time to wait for God to keep His promise.

Perhaps Noah got discouraged at times. He could not see how things were going to turn out, but he kept on doing the job that God had told him to do. Noah is a good example for us to follow when we face tough situations. It is not easy to be jeered at. It is hard to wait a long time for God to do what He has promised, but there are rewards for those who obey Him. Bible stories about Job and Joseph teach us this is so.

God was very patient with the unbelievers. He gave them 120 years while the Ark was being built to see that He meant what He said, to turn from their sins, and to believe Him in order to be saved. But they continued to enjoy their wicked ways. They did not care what would happen to them later on. They did not make the right choice. The Bible describes it this way: "For Christ also died for sins once for all . . . in order that He might bring us to God . . . the patience of God kept waiting in the days of Noah, during the construction of the Ark, in which a few, that is, eight persons, were brought safely through the water" (1 Peter 3:18-20). God wants to help you make the right choices too. He will help you, if you ask Him. Joshua told his people to "choose for yourselves today whom you will serve . . . but as for me and my house, we will serve the Lord" (Joshua 24:15). Have you made the choice to serve the Lord? The story of Noah's obedience to God teaches us the important lesson of choosing to obey and serve Him.

120 years to build the Ark

Chapter 14

Did Dinosaurs Enter the Ark?

The day came when God brought every kind of animal into the Ark. Can you imagine a lion peacefully walking into the Ark with a lamb in front of him? Wouldn't the terrible Tyrannosaurus Rex, as well as bears and wolves, kill and eat harmless animals like kittens and rabbits as they marched toward the Ark? No, not at all! Why not? Because God not only miraculously led the animals into the Ark, but He changed and controlled their natural instincts so they would not be harmful. God knew that Noah could not do that. So God did for Noah what Noah could not do.

When Noah's family and the animals were safely inside the Ark and the door was closed, the Flood began. The Bible says, "on the same day all the fountains of the great deep burst open and the floodgates of the sky were opened" (Genesis 7:11). Probably some of the unbelievers changed their minds about Noah's warnings, but it was too late. Soon they were destroyed by the waters of the Flood.

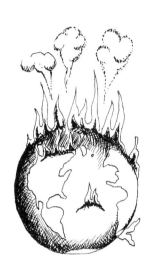

People in our world today are as corrupt as they were in Noah's time. They are doing all sorts of wickedness and violence. God said it would be this way. He has warned people to turn from their sin and believe, because He is going to destroy the earth again. This time the world will be destroyed by fire. A wooden Ark will not save people when the great fire comes. But God has made a way that they can be saved: a wooden cross. Jesus Christ died on the cross to save us from our sins. Then he rose again in victory over death. So

now we can receive God's forgiveness and eternal life by putting our trust in Him.

Did dinosaurs go into the Ark? The Bible says, "Noah and his sons and his wife and his sons' wives with him entered the Ark . . . animals . . . and birds and everything that creeps on the ground . . . went into the Ark . . . as God had commanded" (Genesis 7:7-9). Remember that dinosaurs were great lizards, and lizards are among God's creeping things. So yes, dinosaurs did go into the Ark.

Did two 80-ton Brachiosaurus's really walk into the Ark? Would they not sink the barge? How could they get through the door? Two important facts will help solve this problem. One is the size of the Ark. The other is a secret about dinosaurs.

The Ark was so huge that 520 railroad boxcars could fit inside of it. That is gigantic! It is estimated that about

40,000 animals entered the Ark. Of course there were large animals like giraffes and elephants. But there were also small animals like squirrels, mice and chipmunks. The average size of all the animals was about that of a sheep.

The secret about dinosaurs is that they kept growing as long as they were alive! People do not do that, but some reptiles do.

Perhaps the first thing your grandparents say to you if they have not seen you for a long time is, "How you have grown this year!" If you were a little dinosaur at a dinosaur family reunion, you could look up at your grandpa and say, "Why, grandpa, how you have grown this year!"

Huge dinosaurs were not on the Ark. Old dinosaurs would be grandpas and grandmas that could not have babies. God brought only younger, smaller pairs into the Ark so that when they left the Ark, they could "breed abundantly on the earth" (Genesis 8:17) just as God had planned.

Chapter 15

Conditions Inside the Ark

Have you ever wondered how only eight people could take care of the thousands of animals that were in the Ark? If you have a rabbit hutch, you know how much time it takes to keep it clean. Even a kitty litter box is a chore. And a horse barn really takes effort. Don't you think the Ark could have been very smelly and dirty?

God planned a solution to that problem. Genesis 8:1 says that "God remembered Noah." Does that mean that God was so busy overseeing the Flood that He forgot Noah and his family for a time, and then all of a sudden remembered that they were down there tossing around on the water? Not at all. God never forgets His people or what He has promised to do for them. He always takes care of those who trust in Him. When the Bible says that "God remembered Noah," it means that God took special care of Noah and all his needs.

"God remembered Noah"

But what about the animals? Didn't they need care and feeding? God knew that eight people could not do all the work that 40,000 animals would require, so He had a plan all worked out for them. He would never give Noah's family more work than they could handle.

What probably happened to take care of the problem was this: God led the animals into the Ark and into the compartments that were prepared for them. In those stalls was just the right kind of food for each animal. They ate their food, then God put them to sleep in a condition which we call hibernation.

God had to slow down many of the creatures' natural functions, including reproduction, in order to keep life inside the Ark bearable for Noah and his family for such a long time. If two rabbits had been living under normal conditions, there would have been dozens of rabbits by the time the animals went out of the Ark! The same would be true for mice, mosquitoes and many other creatures. Hibernation would have been one way for God to take care of the needs of the people and the animals on the Ark.

They left the ark two by two.

For 371 days the animals slept quietly in the Ark. That is longer than you wait from one birthday to the next. Thus, God not only remembered Noah, but He also "remembered . . . all the beasts . . . that were with him in the Ark" (Genesis 8:1) and took care of them in a very special way.

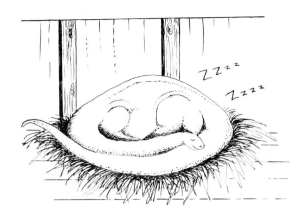

"God took care of them in a special way."

What do you think Noah and his family were doing during those Flood days? Were they curled up on their mats and sleeping all the time? That is doubtful. Perhaps they spent a lot of time praising God that He was protecting them, and praying that God would continue to take care of them. They had so many things to be thankful for. For one thing, God had preserved them from being destroyed with all the other people in the Flood.

Weren't they almost scared to death as the gigantic barge tossed on the raging waters? The Ark probably pitched and rolled a good bit. Perhaps Noah and his family were frightened. But they had trusted God before, and they could trust Him again. Perhaps they said something similar to what David later said: "When I am afraid, I will put my trust in Thee" (Psalm 56:3). Because of God's provisions, they found the Ark to be a safe and peaceful place of refuge.

> "What time
> I am afraid,
> I will trust
> in God."

91

"Then God spoke to Noah, saying. . . bring out with you. . . every creeping thing that creeps on the earth, that they may breed abundantly on the earth."

GENESIS 8:15-17

Chapter 16

Did Dinosaurs Go Out of the Ark?

Then came the day that the Flood was over. The Ark had landed in the mountains of Ararat, which are in modern-day Turkey. The ground finally became dry enough for the animals to walk out of the Ark (Genesis 8:14). Did dinosaurs go out of the Ark, or did they die in there before the Flood ended? The Bible says that Noah's family and "every beast, every creeping thing, and every bird, everything that moves upon the earth went out . . . from the Ark" (Genesis 8:18, 19). So yes, every animal that went into the Ark came out of it when the Flood was over.

What a sight! Birds fluttering out in droves, insects buzzing and crawling out by the thousands, animals leaping and frolicking about, and all kinds of creeping things lumbering down the gangplank! They must have been full of energy after sleeping for more than a year!

Before the dino-
saurs walked out of
the Ark, they may
have eaten a good
meal to strengthen
them. They began to
scatter over the sur-
face of the earth to
multiply and fill the
earth again as God
had commanded them
to do (Genesis 8:17).

But soon the violent characteristics of the flesh-eaters
returned. They could not get along on vegetation, so they
returned to their carnivorous ways. Those flesh-eating
characteristics are with them to this day, but there will come
one more time when animals will be tame and will not hurt
each other or people. When our Lord establishes His
kingdom on the earth, "the wolf and the lamb shall graze
together . . . they shall do no evil or harm" (Isaiah 65:25).

Noah and his family must have been very glad to walk
on land again. Noah did not forget to thank God for his
loving care. "Then Noah built an altar to the Lord, and took

of every clean animal and of every clean bird and offered burnt offerings on the altar" (Genesis 8:20). God expects us to remember to thank Him for taking tender loving care of us. The Bible commands, "In everything give thanks, for this is God's will for you" (1 Thessalonians 5:18). Thank Him for His Word that teaches us about the dinosaurs.

"The earth will wear out like a garment, and its inhabitants will die in like manner."

ISAIAH 51:6

Part Five

THE END OF DINOSAURS

"We know that the whole creation groans and suffers the pains of childbirth together until now."

ROMANS 8:22

Chapter 17

What Happened to the Dinosaurs?

What happened to those mysterious monsters that once roamed our earth? For about 1,600 years after Creation week, people and animals populated the earth. Then came the Flood. But God preserved His creation by providing an Ark that saved one family, as well as every kind of air-breathing animal. After the Flood this little group of people and animals began to replenish the earth as God had planned.

When they walked out of the Ark, the dinosaurs saw a very different world than the one they were used to. High rugged mountain ranges, like the Alps and the Himalayas, appeared where there had been much lower mountains before. Deep canyons had been dug into the soft earth by fast-moving water. That is how the Grand Canyon was formed. Shallow expanses of ocean water became the deep basins of today.

Perhaps before the Flood there were more land areas, and more space for plants and animals. After the Flood, plants did not grow as large, and they were less abundant.

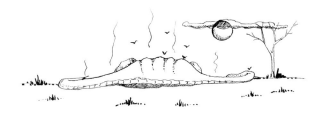

Many starved to death.

Also, there were fewer swamp lands, and deserts began to appear, so some dinosaurs could not get their favorite foods. Because of this shortage of food, many dinosaurs starved to death. As the herbivores died, so did the carnivores that preyed on them.

The radiation from the sun began to destroy living things, because the harmful rays were no longer blocked out by the vapor canopy. As a result, the life span of plants and animals was gradually shortened.

The climate of the world changed drastically after the Flood. No longer was it warm and humid all over the world. Some areas were severely cold. Perhaps some of the dinosaurs could not adjust to this change, so they froze to death.

New diseases may have caused the extinction of dinosaurs as well as other animals. This is happening today. In 1964 a disease called avian pox was brought to Hawaii from Nepal. This sickness has brought about the near extinction of one of Hawaii's most unusual birds, the 'alala. Experts believe that many kinds of animals are becoming extinct every year from starvation, disease, or man's destruction.

Man is the biggest killer of animals today. He is causing the extinction of the African elephant by killing them by the thousands for their ivory tusks, which are made into jewelry and other beautiful ornaments. In the late 18th century, 'o'o birds were killed in Hawaii to make a yellow feather cape for the King, Kamehameha. Scientists know of only one 'o'o bird today. Perhaps man aided in the destruction of dinosaurs by hunting them to extinction thousands of years ago.

Some men try to make us believe that a huge object from outer space splashed into the ocean, causing the extinction of some marine creatures. They also say that later, something else struck our planet, causing the dinosaurs to die out. The Bible says nothing about this; but it does center our attention on the greatest catastrophe of all: the Genesis Flood.

Why would God create such a spectacular animal as the mighty dinosaur, only to allow him to die out? The Bible does not give an answer, except to say that God's creation of the huge, creeping reptiles shows how powerful He is.

Thousands of animals — saber-toothed cats, mastodons, mammoths, huge ground sloths, short-faced bears, and dire wolves — have become extinct. We do not give them much thought, but we ask many questions about the dinosaur because his enormous size fascinates us.

We still hear reports that living dinosaurs have been seen on the earth. Natives of the Congo in West Central Africa describe dinosaur-type creatures that they have seen in the jungles. In 1977 Japanese fishermen pulled the remains of what they thought was a huge reptile out of the South Pacific Ocean. We need to wait for more scientific evidence before we can be sure about these reports.

Chapter 18

Dinosaurs Today

Although the giant reptiles died out, some smaller ones are still living today. It is not certain why they have survived. Perhaps they were able to adapt to the changed world. We call these animals "small" because we are comparing them to dinosaurs that weighed many tons. However, some of these creeping survivors weigh hundreds of pounds.

THE KOMODO DRAGON

On the lonely Indonesian island of Komodo prowls the world's largest lizard — the Komodo Dragon Lizard. Komodo is in the south Pacific Ocean. Only about one thousand of these mysterious reptiles are living today.

Komodo Dragons look like the dragons in medieval drawings. The only thing missing is fire spewing out of their nostrils!

The Komodo Dragon's dark, shiny hide looks like polished black gravel. He has long, sharp claws and an armour-plated head. His foot-long, forked tongue resembles the tongue of a snake as it flicks in and out of his mouth. He probably uses it to smell and touch what he is going to eat.

Komodo Dragons grow to be nine feet long and weigh about 300 pounds. They feed on the carcasses of dead animals such as deer, wild pigs, goats and water buffalo. Even though the adult dragon lizards are slow and clumsy, they still hunt live animals when the opportunity arises. The young ones probably eat snakes, geckos and bird eggs, as well as dead animals.

An adult Komodo Dragon Lizard eats like a power shovel. He rips big pieces from a carcass and gulps them down — bones, hair, bugs and all. If he is scared by an intruder, he can swallow an entire meal at once. The bite of the Komodo Dragon is poisonous, as well. He bites and infects his prey, then waits for it to die. His feeding habits can be savage. At other times, however, he seems sluggish and disinterested in eating or fighting.

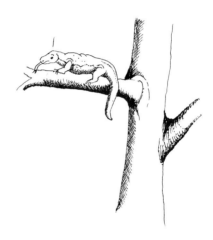

While the full-grown lizards lumber along the ground at a rather slow pace, the young ones are as nimble as monkeys. They are so agile that they make excellent tree climbers. People have not studied the habits of the Komodo Dragon Lizard very much, so there is a lot about them that remains a great mystery.

THE MONA IGUANA

On a very small island in the Caribbean lives a very large lizard. If you saw him, you would think that you were looking at some mythical beast designed by the ancient Egyptians. He is called the Mona iguana, because he lives on the little bean-shaped island of Mona. Mona is situated midway between Puerto Rico and the Dominican Republic.

The Mona iguana has stocky legs, an unusually short

tail, and an enormous body with lots of wrinkles. His massive head is covered with large bumps. A horn on his snout gives him a ferocious appearance.

Even though this extraordinary creature looks fierce, he is not harmful to humans or other animals. He is chiefly a plant-eater. One of his favorite foods is the manchineel fruit that can cause serious sickness and even death to humans. Eating is not a daily requirement for the Mona iguana.

How does a Mona iguana spend his waking hours? About ninety-five percent of the day he rests, spending a good bit of his time underground. Underground living spares him from fights, keeps his body temperature even, and conserves his precious body water and energy.

Rests 95% of his day-- HOW LAZY!

THE GALAPAGOS TORTOISE

Have you ever had the fun of riding on a huge Galapagos tortoise at a zoo? If you have, you can tell your friends that you have ridden on a reptile! This huge turtle looks like a walking boulder as he clunks over the black volcanic rocks of Isabela Island in the Pacific Ocean. Isabela is one of the Galapagos Islands, 600 miles west of the South American country of Ecuador.

These domed reptiles are known as the heavyweights among the world's cold-blooded land animals. Males can eventually weigh up to 600 pounds. Females seldom weigh as much as 300 pounds. They can live to be 150 years old.

Galapagos tortoises are peaceful, but they are very curious and very strong. Once a group of people went to the Galapagos Islands to observe them. One 450-pound creature ripped open their tent door, devoured their socks and underwear, and smashed a five-gallon steel can while he was noseying around.

The Galapagos tortoise leads a lazy life overall. He sleeps about sixteen hours each day. He wakes up at about seven or eight o'clock in the morning, then basks in the sun for a couple of hours while his bulky body warms up. During the rest of the day he may travel only a few hundred yards in search of a meal.

This giant eats a variety of foods that seem very strange to us. He gorges himself on stinging nettles and prickly pear fruit. Like the Mona iguana, he likes fruits that are poisonous to men.

The tortoise retires at four or five o'clock in the afternoon. To keep himself warm during the night, he burrows halfway into the mud. The mud also protects him from mosquitoes. The next day the mud dries on his body, protecting him from little ticks and bugs that like to burrow into his skin.

If a tick does manage to get into his long, wrinkled neck or his head or legs, the turtle stretches out so that little ground finches can peck them off. God has programmed many animals to help each other in this way.

Do you remember reading in Chapter Three that animals cannot think like people do? They function on instinct which their Creator God has programmed into them. The nesting habits of the female Galapagos tortoise is only one of the thousands of examples of God's wonderful design of instinct. For about five hours the female tortoise excavates, measures and shapes a hole. Then, in about twenty minutes, she lays up to seventeen eggs. After the last egg has been laid, she rearranges them into a single layer across the bottom of the hole. Over the tops of the eggs she packs a layer of mud to keep them warm during the night and cool during the day. It takes the eggs from three to eight months to hatch, depending on the temperature.

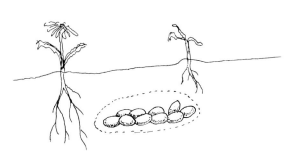

A baby turtle struggles for one to five days to break out of the egg. Then he must claw his way out of the hardened mud nest. He can usually do this in a few weeks, yet a little hatchling cannot wait weeks for food. What keeps him from starving to death? God has provided a yolk sac that is attached to the baby's belly. This sac will provide food for

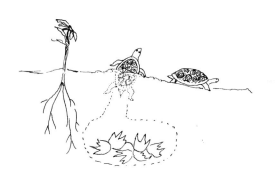

him as long as seven months if he should need it. Then at last he is free to charge about like a little three-ounce bulldozer!

In the past, men have killed the Galapagos turtles for their oil and meat. They killed many more than they could use. Today there are laws against their slaughter. Now dogs, cats, rats, goats and other animals devour the hatchlings. Pigs dig up their nests. A warden said that "one pig can destroy dozens of nests in a night and not miss an egg." The Galapagos tortoise is one of the thousands of animals that are becoming extinct.

Chapter 19

If Skeletons Could Talk

If the skeletons of extinct dinosaurs could talk, they might say something like this to you: "We have all died out. When we died, that was the end of us. We had no soul. When you die, that will not be the end of you, because you do have a soul."

Jesus saves and keeps us.

Are you afraid to die? You do not have to be afraid. Jesus Christ died on the cross and shed His blood to wash away your sin. Then He rose from the grave to prove that He was truly God. If you believe that He died for you, tell Him so. Ask Him to cleanse your heart from sin. Then when you die, you can go to Heaven.

Heaven is a wonderful place. It is God's home, and Jesus is getting it ready for you. He promised, "In my Father's house are many dwelling places . . . I go to prepare a place for you . . . I will come again and receive you to myself; that where I am, there you may be also" (John 14:2, 3). Sin has spoiled our earth and made it a very unhappy place. In Heaven there will be no sin, no sickness, no sorrow, pain, death, nor anything to hurt or harm you. Best of all, Jesus, the One who loves you, will be there with you forever.

INDEX

"Worship Him who made the heavens and the earth and sea..."

REVELATION 14:7